marriage enrichment

edited by Paul F. Wilczak Ph.D.

ABBEY PRESS
St. Meinrad, Indiana 47577

The five chapters of this book originally appeared as articles in the *In-Depth* Series, "Marriage Enrichment," published in the February 1979 through June 1979 issues of *MARRIAGE and Family Living* magazine. They are here copyrighted as a collection in slightly revised form.

The review of Pope John Paul II's book, *Love and Responsibility*, first appeared in the March, 1979 issue of *MARRIAGE and Family Living*.

PHOTOS: Bob Smith, Cover; Camerique, pages 4 and 12; Major Morris, page 26; Strix Pix, pages 40 and 61; Florence Sharp, page 52; Jean-Claude Lejeune, pages 66 and 75.

Library of Congress Card Number
79-53514
ISBN 0-87029-155-6

© 1979 St. Meinrad Archabbey
St. Meinrad, Indiana 47577

CONTENTS

	Introduction	5
I	The Fullness of Physical Love **Paul F. Wilczak**	13
II	Intellectual Growth and Intimacy **Mary G. Durkin**	27
III	Emotional Growth in Marriage **Ken and Becky Eggeman**	41
IV	Spiritual Growth in Marriage **Gordon Lester**	53
V	Parenting and Marital Love: When Is It Good Enough? **Arthur Mandelbaum**	67
	Questions for Reflection and Discussion	79
	A Review of Pope John Paul II's book on Christian Marriage **Paul F. Wilczak**	83
	Suggested Readings	93

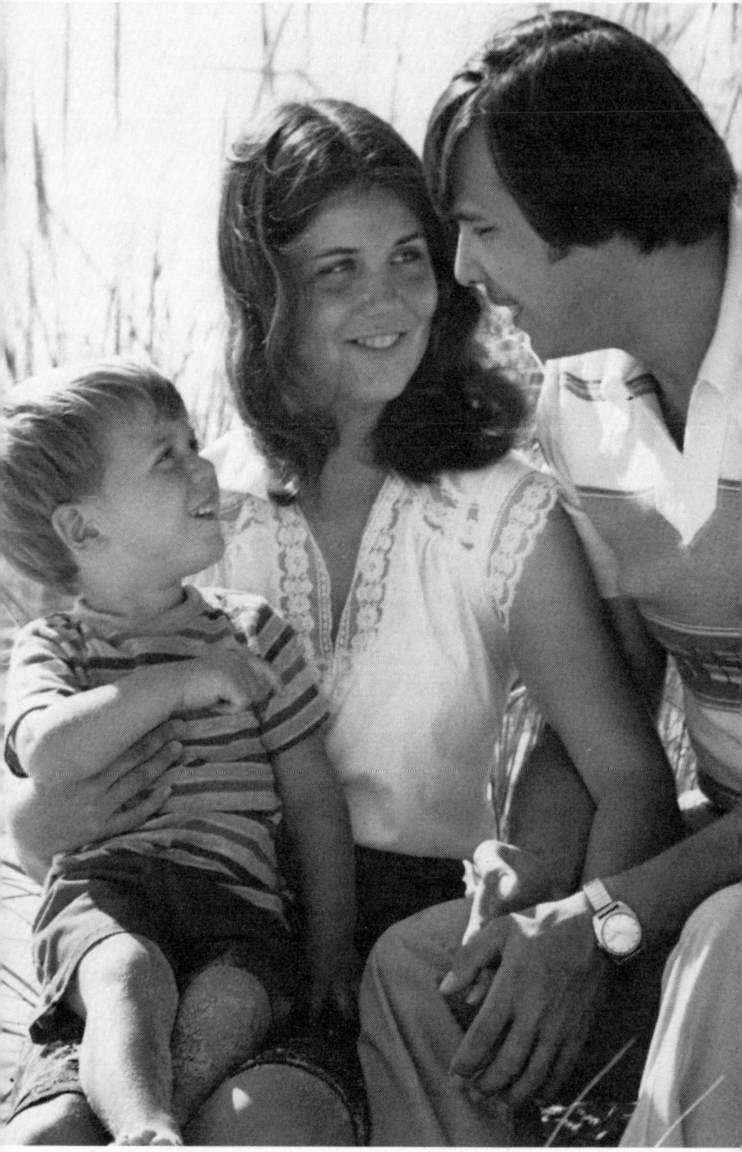

Introduction

This collection of articles on marriage enrichment has been prepared with several purposes in mind. The collection could be subtitled "Support and Growth in Marital Relating," for the communication of support to married couples is a primary purpose of this book. To provide signposts and guidelines toward marital growth is another major purpose. A third goal is to make available valuable knowledge of key areas in married life. The latter is especially important to Roman Catholics in view of the concerted effort of the Catholic Church in the United States to develop ministries to families. Among these ministries the American bishops have specifically included ministry for married couples. This book can serve as a significant resource for persons involved in that ministry.

Ministry for married couples is my own

central professional concern and deep personal interest. Many of the things I have found helpful in my work have been brought together here for your benefit. They are meant to challenge and stimulate you and may evoke both agreement and disagreement. But that is their usefulness. We must all take a fresh look at marriage today. It is time to challenge our preconceptions, to explore our convictions, and to renew and deepen our values.

I chose to edit and to contribute to this book for two reasons. The first is to point out that in our society marriage needs support as a way of life and a Christian calling. The second is to suggest a number of ways to grow in marriage. These two reasons stem from the two complementary aspects of ministry for married couples. One aspect of this ministry is *to* married couples. It is a supportive and challenging going out to others. The second is a ministry *in* marriage, of spouse to spouse, which does not intentionally reach out to help other married couples.

My first reason, emphasizing the need to support marriage in our society, is important because real support for marriages hardly exists in America today. This may seem to be an incredible statement in view of tax breaks, marriage laws, public pieties about marriage, church programs, and the like. But in spite of the fact that more people marry today than ever before, the couples who marry are largely left on their own to sink or swim. Marriages are supported by legal, economic, and educational institutions, but rarely experience the ongoing emotional, personal, spiritual, and communal support they need. Consequently, in the mainstream of American life twenty-five to thirty-five percent of marriages sink. Perhaps as many others barely stay afloat or merely tread water. And the number of divorces is likely to continue to increase, as it has from year to year for more than a decade.

Any alternative to this decline in the staying power of marriages would hinge on one factor. This single factor is both simple yet frustratingly difficult to actualize. This factor is the couple's appreciation of the value of their marriage to the community around them (of which they are a part) and that community's real celebration of the couple's marriage through the years, not only at the wedding. What this one factor implies theologically makes it describable not only as "difficult" but "impossible." The conversion, commitment, and gift of self necessitated by this factor make it a realization of grace, not merely a work of nature. Human beings can not accomplish this task unaided. And that is very basic theology. It is also very basic theology that God loves us first and is at work ahead of our efforts in a hidden yet powerful way. In the New Testament this was symbolized by the expression "the Reign of God." The Reign of God was the context of the proclamation of Jesus. It is also the context of the gospel today but in the sense of God's real personal presence. The symbolic expression is not merely a scriptural ornament to preaching. God draws human beings into relationships in which love will be effective in some humanly comprehensible way. This is the context of God's caring, and through its reaching into human lives the spouses are offered the context of effective, mutual support which they need.

But theology must be brought down to earth, expressed in ordinary language, and made experiential. In our society many married couples struggle along without support and perhaps without even much awareness of the grace they are waiting for. They may think of themselves as not having enough friends, social status, money, or luck. They may feel unhappy, dissatisfied, or bored, and hide these feelings behind an "all-OK," happy public image. But, as over a million divorces indicated in 1978, human efforts can last only so long. After that they become statistics which in turn serve to hide the painful human feelings involved.

I would not want to reduce this issue of increasing divorce entirely to a matter of the lack of support for marriages. But I do believe that lack to be a highly significant factor. We see marriages eroding in our society, but not because there is no grace which could generate a communal context for effective support. Our faith affirms that God is at work out there. What interferes is a weak sense of communal responsibility for the meaning and value of marriage, a sense which can evoke the gift of self necessary for cooperation with God's grace. Pope John Paul II expressed this sense well when he said in his book, *Love and Responsibility,* "the gift of self as a form of love is shaped within the person on the basis of a mature vision of value and on the readiness of a person's strength of will to become involved . . ." This applies both to married persons and to those who witness their marriages. And to witness a marriage means to become involved in its meaning and value by sustaining, nurturing, and challenging real married persons in a deeply personal way. It means actively entering their lives with respectful initiative.

But our own superficial or merely intellectual beliefs can interfere with such witness or they can block us from awareness of our responsibility for such witness. One such belief is the view that marital love is fundamentally a matter of private significance. I see this belief as common in our society and as a fundamental reason effective support for marriages has not materialized in spite of available resources. As a consequence, the reality of many marriages remains hidden behind a public facade, an attempt to look good. This pseudomutuality can be maintained unless the couple splits up. In that event offhand comments may be uttered such as, "How could it have happened? They seemed to have everything!" or "There must have been something *wrong with them.*" Such casual remarks reveal an attitude of non-involvement or merely passive witnessing. What is needed, however, is active witnessing, involvement, in plain English *giving a damn* about marriage as a symbol of love, human and divine.

But the problem is in our cultural context, not simply in the married couples who fail or in the witnesses who merely watch them fall apart. Marriages cannot grow in a private vacuum. And marriages which do not grow will die. But the renewal which will permit growth in marital love will be in the experience of witness connecting couple and community in loving involvement. This will change the cultural context and transform it through the power of the gift of self.

My second reason for editing this book also touches upon this notion of witness. This is the ministry of *growth in marriage*. Spouses deeply involved with one another, even though not explicitly intending involvement with others in a ministry to them, *are witnessing*. Their loving, growing marriages are a kind of *eucharist* in their own neighborhoods—in the meaning of the Greek *eu charis*, a *good gift*—to all who touch their lives. The open spontaneity of their love furnishes a light of hope and faith as well. People who encounter them and who are not seriously afflicted by the competitiveness and one-up-manship so common in our culture can say, "Yes, somehow it is possible. The gift of love can be more than a childish dream. Perhaps it can touch our lives too."

In a way, this book is a witness to that possibility. Love, growth, involvement, and enrichment can be real. But they need to be worked on, thought through, and continually relearned and renewed. The authors who have contributed to this volume have combined their efforts to help you with this challenge. They comment on the different social contexts of marital growth and enrichment—the sexual, the intellectual, the emotional, the spiritual, and the relational. In addition to this, I have included my review of Pope John Paul II's book on marriage, *Love and Responsibility*. In it his own statements are quoted at length in my own translation to provide you with an additional source of enrichment.

Our hope in publishing this short book is that you will find in the efforts of these authors new alternatives for your own marriage. Moreover, we hope you read the message between the lines: Your marriage is important to us. It makes a difference to us if you succeed or fail. And more important yet, your marriage means something to everyone around you. Make it count for them and for yourselves.

Paul F. Wilczak, Ph.D.

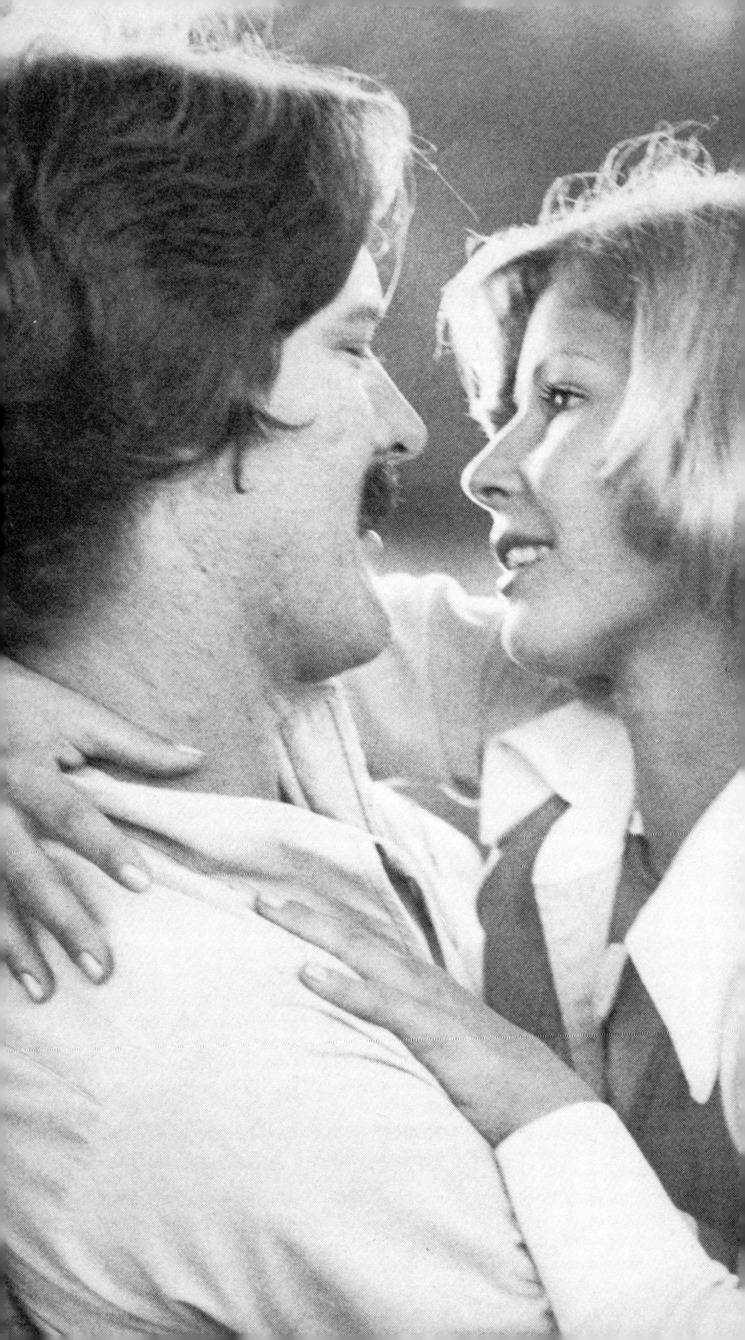

I
The Fullness of Physical Love
Paul F. Wilczak

Paul F. Wilczak, Ph.D. is a member of the staff of the Center for Pastoral Ministry of the Catholic Diocese of Kansas City-St. Joseph, MO. He is enrolled at the Menninger Foundation in the Family Therapy Training Program for Community Practitioners. He lives with his wife, Priscilla, and son, Sean, in Kansas City.

To understand what the sexual relationship implied by marriage means to us today it is essential, I believe, to examine what commercials are telling us about ourselves. Many new products are presented as an integral part of an intimate relationship that they serve to enhance. These overall "packages" are daily becoming more elegant and sophisticated: the lady has legs men notice; the man's face is smooth to the touch; wine spans the gap between them; and the tractor mower saves our energy for other activity. The hallmarks of the sales package are richness, luxury, sophistication, competence, and youthful potency. These are combined in various proportions to create a media image unified by sexuality: total man, total woman, totally relating. And it has been created because we buy it: that is the way we like to see ourselves.

Yet there is something missing in this "total" picture. Sexuality generates a tension of opposites by being both enticing and threatening. As an urge or drive it can bring a dynamic excitement, but it can also be frustratingly overpowering. In interpersonal relationships it can enhance the enthusiasm of free dedication or be wielded as an enslaving weapon. Sex is power and, as power, can be creative and destructive. Its negative aspects are largely and intentionally omitted from the "total" package. They would interfere with sales. This omission gives the package a kind of unreality which we can see if we take a closer look. It is interesting to note, however, that the negative side also appears in isolation elsewhere on the scene. The threatening aspects of sex are the focus of many traditional religious groups. Some go so far as to use the word *sin* primarily to mean *sexual sin*.

Both extremes disturb a balance I consider crucial to human and to religious development. In my view sex should be accepted as both threatening and creative. These two aspects are also characteristics of "the holy." And this is why sex can symbolize the holy; the emotional impact of both combines the same elements; both are at once enticing and threatening. This possibility is crucial to marriage as a religious vocation. But our culture presents the holy and sex as in conflict with each other. This is rooted in our deep fear that one will submerge or even destroy the other.

Let's take a closer look at this drastic conflict. Consider sexuality as presented by media advertising. The enticing aspect of sex functions here as a commercially available substitute for the attractive aspect of the holy, as a means to instantaneous ecstasy. The immediate satisfaction of sexual excitement operates as an ultimate, supplanting religious experience. And the media gives you the chance to buy into this ecstasy for the price of a deodorant on sale!

One of the major tasks in this commercialization is to create a sense of great need in the public. It is this need which, when successfully evoked and yoked by advertising, transforms the public into consumers. The need in this case is often presented as the severe deprivation foisted on the public by Christian inhibition and prudery. This is done by innuendo, sophisticated pleading, or hostile blaming. The message is the same: "This magic commodity offers you the key out of a sad world of deprivation and into a realm of sheer delight!" This marketing approach lowers religion itself to the level of another product competing with the sex package but marked, "Hazardous to Your Health."

But let us go a step further and take a look at why commercial ventures which go beyond TV and magazine commercials by packaging sex as sex (rather than perfume as sexy) have prospered. What I have in mind are the more "respectable" products in the magazine and book trade such as *Playboy, Penthouse, Playgirl,* and *Forum,* plus a wide variety of erotic books for the "sensuous" man, woman, or couple. A product line catches on because it corresponds with some felt need among consumers. Now this need can be hyped up or twisted to fit the purposes of the marketers. But it cannot be created from nothing. The need must in some way really exist in order to be manipulated into a profitable venture. In the case of soft-core pornography the need is based on the fact that human sexual satisfaction and competence are not simply instinctual matters but require social affirmation and support. In addition, there is also a human need for fantasy in attaining sexual satisfaction. The latter is sometimes expressed by the saying that the most important human sex organ is the brain.

I would like to consider the second need first because it is more obvious and closer to the experience of most people. Imagination is essential for all creative and recreative endeavors. Fantasy is necessary for sexual satisfaction because it undergirds all human satisfaction. Dissatisfaction is rooted in the insufficiency of a given factual situation. Such dissatisfaction spurs our creativity to transcend the factual imaginatively. While the eye sees from but one angle, imagination spins the perceived before the mind's eye to reveal unseen facets and explores their hidden possibilities. Creative human fantasy takes the given as a cue to move from what is to what could be.

For instance, imagination functions in motivating couples to marry. They imaginatively transcend their singleness by fantasizing married life together. This enables them to move beyond the factual into a more satisfactory, richer life. There is, of course, a risk and a danger involved in any imaginative leap. The nonfactual future may be no richer or even be poorer than the present. There's no getting around this risk. And the danger is that the fantasy may be merely an escape from realities and an irresponsible flight into an endless series of new images. For example, such a flight may represent a person's quest for a perfect sexual partner. The reality which is fled in this way is the fact that the person searching for a better partner really contributed to all the sexual failure left behind. And the hard truth is that failure will likely be repeated with someone else because fantasy is masking personal responsibility. So the fantasy goes round and round, hardly ever touching ground.

The other need, the human need for social affirmation and support in the attaining of sexual competence and satisfaction, is, in my view, more significant. This is true because the need is largely ignored in our society. Consequently, I believe it is the more powerful motivator in the consumption of erotic commodities. The need is ignored and the support not provided because, among other things, of our mistaken belief that sex is primarily instinctual behavior. Even among primates such is not the case, let alone among human beings. Animal studies have underscored the necessity of social learning and affirmation for attaining sexual maturity. Since this is true for the rhesus monkey, a creature much more instinctual than we are, it may even be *more* true of us.

In my opinion this unmet need serves as the entree for the "playboy" marketing expert. He offers a feeling of pseudosupport. In flaunting his circulation, exploiting his notoriety, and disseminating his trademark, he tells those in need of social affirmation and support that everyone is pulsating to the "playboy" beat while he alone calls the tunes. But there is no actual, interpersonal support and affirmation given—only a counterfeit substitute. Just as the companionship TV offers merely masks the loneliness of its isolated viewer, the support of the publishers of erotic materials is also illusory. They may claim to be the champions of your erotic freedom but in reality are in the business to make money.

An alternative to the total commodity approach would be to develop a way to provide *real* satisfaction of the need that keeps the erotic presses rolling. I shall call this alternative "supporting the spiritual carnality of Christian marriage." This could be a significant route to marriage enrichment. But as a real alternative it cannot merely provide a new competing product. A real alternative must go beyond the marketplace into the realm of actual, mutual, social support; it must be based on mutual relations as a life process. Books and magazines, no matter how true their contents, cannot be supportive. Only people can affirm other people. And in my belief such affirmation can develop only within the context of a religious group of people.

Thus, we have returned to the holy but, surprisingly, also to the pornographically erotic. There is a hidden religious quality to the pornographic products on the market. In a basic sense this quality stems from their communication of the ideal of sexual ecstasy as an ultimate concern. We have here an idolatry in an age without gods, Venus minus her temple. But the comparison applies further. A significant feature of current erotic publications is their personal accounts of physical sexual encounters sent in by readers. The social support intended by this practice is fairly clear. Less clear, however, is their ritual quality. They often depict sexual encounters with strangers in commercial public places such as bars, stores, airplanes, hotels, etc. These stories read very much like ancient accounts of ritual prostitution in public temples in which the stranger-priest symbolized the divine.

The ritual quality comes from the stopping of time in the stories, which often take place *after hours* in a store or bar. This detail creates a poetic effect of timelessness. And the formalizing of sexual release with no thought or possibility of conception stops human time in another way. Here we can see an implicit denial of deaths of the sexual partners. It is as if their youth, beauty, potency, and excitement could never die. There is a manic aura to the excited coupling which I believe is motivated by a flight from death anxiety. The characters copulate like immortals eternally joining and rejoining.

Take these accounts out of their ritual frames and put them within a real context of relationships and their grotesqueness emerges. This happens because the stories are ritually framed to exclude the rationality of sexual life and deeper personal commitments. Here we can see how the negative or threatening side of sexuality is carefully hidden. Real relationships do threaten us with pain from the work of growing and the possibility of loss. The easy-come/easy-go quality of pornography simply can't be real or really sustain life. It does, however, sell books and magazines (and fat advertising contracts).

Marriage as an explicitly religious way of

life presents an entirely different picture. First, in the religiously committed intimacy of marriage a distinction is made between the truly mysterious and the merely new and unknown. Marital intimacy is open to the stranger within the familiar loved one, not the stranger picked up on the outside. In saying this I am contradicting psychologist C.A. Tripp, who believes that sexual interest dissolves with increasing marital intimacy. Such a belief can be used to rationalize hitting the bars or having a string of affairs. What he's talking about is pseudomutuality, not intimacy. In plain English, that's getting into the rut of constantly looking for a new thrill. Genuine intimacy means transcending stereotyped familiarity not forever starting all over. It means discovering the ever new depths of the spouse and, in a religious sense, comprehending those depths as a window to the infinite God symbolized by the marital relationship.

Second, the unreality of timeless, death-denying, constantly repeated rituals that go nowhere is replaced with truly mutual relating, responsive to the realities of personal identity and lasting fidelity. Fidelity has long been characterized by the adjective "marital." And many people today presume this to be stifling. Fidelity would be suffocating if considered a requirement imposed from the outside, especially in a legal sense. In its more comprehensive meaning, however, fidelity is a vital human capacity which flows from a person's sense of who he or she is. It depends on a sense of personal identity and faith in self which implies responsibility for taking a certain limited path in life and sticking to it. For people with a strong sense of identity, time is more than clock time; it is the emerging of a unique personal history which is rooted, develops, and culminates in death as a fulfillment. Marriage can be a vital aspect of this history as a loving, caring, creative venture. Spontaneous physical love is an important part of this venture and expresses personal needs, values, and patterns of delightful worldly beauty. But as every married person knows, such spontaneous impulses are not restricted to one's marriage partner. This is normal, natural, and helps make life nicely interesting. But the boundaries of marital responsibility mark off others as beyond the limits of one's life path. New, beautiful, exciting, and attractive people cross our paths every day. A significant number of them could be wonderful sexual partners. Yet in real existence there is one who is chosen in spite of the exciting, self-fulfilling possibilities of all the others, for only through exclusive lasting commitment to one can human love reach its culmination. Intimacy is a matter of depth, not breadth; how truly we know one, not how many we have gotten to know.

In the acceptance of this renunciation, marriage is quite comparable to celibacy. But the vital difference from celibacy is what marks the third aspect of marriage as a religious way of life. In marriage, isolated attributes and physical endowments enhance, for the spouse, the human person with whom bodily intimacy is enjoyed within the religious marital commitment. And by *commitment* I mean the acceptance of mutual, *personal* bonds. Without this transformation the secular partner is merely one who *has* what it takes to turn the knower on. Should someone lose what it takes, the physical bond is broken. But the break merely opens the hairline crack of alienation separating the sex partners from the beginning. They were never truly "two in one flesh." When this is true, it is persons rather than their private parts that make the crucial contact. Physical detail is then transformed into a married wholeness greater than the sum of the parts. Nevertheless, the contact of the persons is also very physical, sexual, and carnal, but in a oneness of spirit expressing a shared life. This is *spiritual carnality,* not something esoteric, abstract, or pietistic, but the actual union of sexual powers and personal meaning in cooperative life. This union *forms across time spent together* in real personal contact, the minutes and hours of everyday life, the ordinary and the very special experiences. Thus, bodily life transforms and grows in mutuality.

This transformation, however, does not come to be easily or in some automatic, instinctual way. Since spiritual carnality is by definition a transcending of instinctual, physical sexuality, it requires something *more.* The nature of that *plus* is suggested by Dr. Claude Lanctot, who is Associate Professor of Community Medicine at the University of Sherbrooke, Quebec. He has spoken of the crucial function of the support of other couples in attaining the sexual mastery necessary for natural family planning. This involves couples forming a support group in which they share and affirm one another's marriages. In such a context the lives of otherwise isolated married couples are transformed into a communal life by the spirit of the group. Sexual mastery no longer remains an individual struggle against the flesh. This same approach can be used to affirm limiting the number of children, increasing their number, or deepening carnal intimacy and responsiveness. This may even be the only way the impact of the media can be overcome. The coming together of a small group of married couples who really care for one another enough to extend to each other mutual support in affirming personal sexuality with the guidance of experienced leaders may be the only answer. It is not something to buy or sell, but a courageous living of the Gospel of God incarnate.

And *incarnate* implies *carnality*, but a carnality which expresses the delicate balance of the spirit of faith, hope, and love. It must seek to be a carnality without covetousness, shame, and guilt—a carnality which reverences and celebrates marital boundaries. Consequently, it would depend on God's gracious support and would fail as a purely human project. In this celebration the group could deepen their appreciation of the Creator's working in the world, working through them in a sexy, bodily, carnal way. In this spiritual-social context fantastic sex becomes the total affirmation of self and other in spousal relationship.

By "fantastic sex" I do not simply mean "Wow! Great! Ecstatic!" Marital sex can be that, but what allows the peaks to be touched is the loving play of fantasy across the being of the beloved. And there is a social side to romantic fantasy which is crucial to private love-making. When a couple gets together with other couples who are close friends to celebrate the gift of life and love (which is what every party is essentially about), each spouse is *pleased* with *all* that is "delightful to behold" and *thrilled* by the many faceted splendor of the spectacle of human complementarity, but each will respond by *giving expression* to this pleasure through the giving-yielding of exclusively committed intimacy that is Christian marriage.

In this social experience there is a symbolizing of the source of all beauty and attractiveness, of the fire which does not consume the people within its realm. In such a community there is living and growing which participates and points at the Creator of life, sex, and every physical beauty and strength. The God from whom the riches of marriage ever flow thus reveals his presence among us.

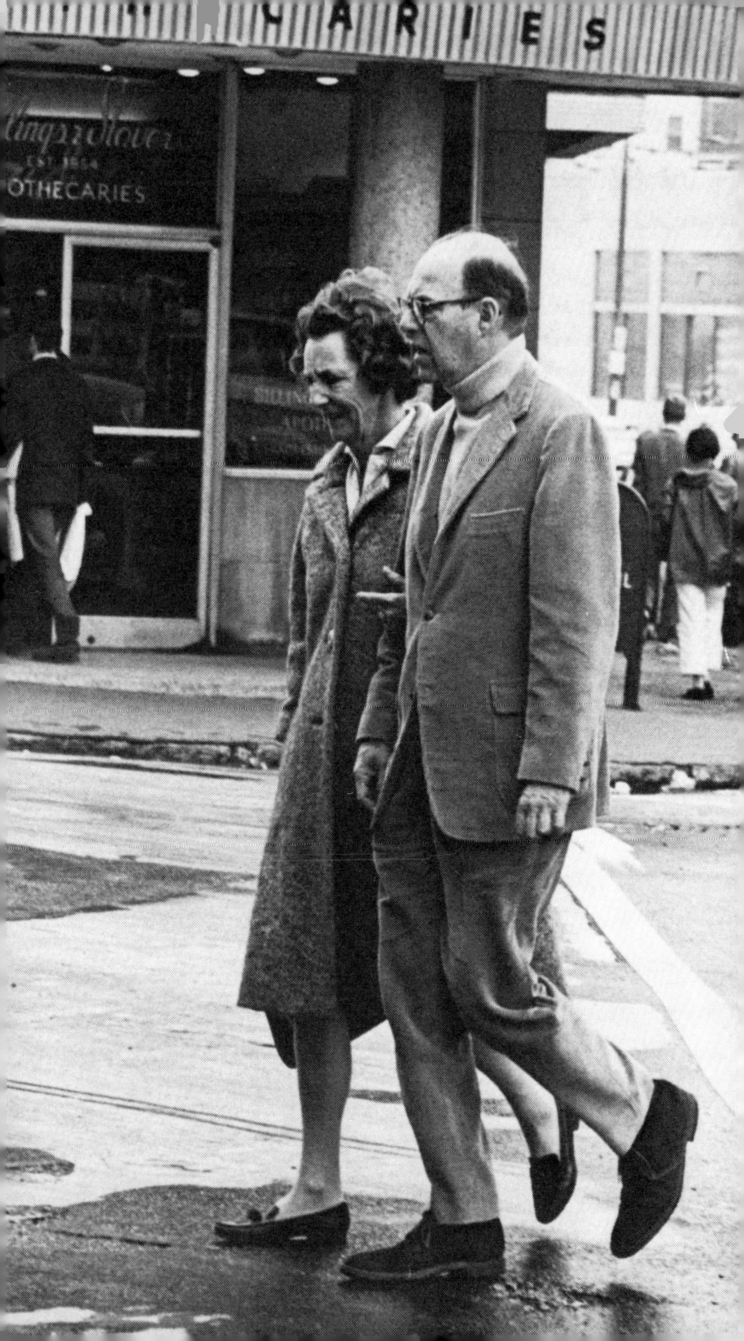
CARIES
OTHECARIES

II
Intellectual Growth and Intimacy

Mary G. Durkin

Mary G. Durkin, D.Mn. is an instructor at the Institute of Pastoral Studies, Loyola University, Chicago. She is a member of the Catholic Theological Society of America and has written and lectured widely. She is married and the mother of seven children.

Among the wives' tales of what to avoid in marriage is the story of the young woman who drops out of school to support her husband while he completes his education. After acquiring the coveted medical, law, or other professional degree, he becomes quite involved in his career while she settles down to raising the family. At some time, perhaps fifteen or twenty years after the wedding, he discovers that his wife has failed to "keep up" with him intellectually. Thus, he turns to a woman with whom he "has more in common." A newer tale, which also alludes to the problems of intellectual incompatability, tells of the thirty-five-year-old wife who returns to college, becomes intellectually stimulated, and discovers that her husband has no desire for intellectual growth beyond what he acquired many years before in school.

Both of these stories are extreme, but they do highlight an increasingly important problem area in marriages in advanced technological societies. Marriage partners who have increased leisure time and longer life spans are confronted with the opportunity for greater growth and intimacy in their marital unions. Intellectual growth is one dimension of human growth, and intellectual stimulation and communication are avenues for developing intimacy. Unfortunately, there has been little attention to this aspect of the marital relationship, and many couples fail to realize that intellectual growth for both partners is a necessary ingredient for a successful or intimate union.

A consideration of the importance of intellectual growth to the maintenance of a good marriage requires that we investigate the roots of the difficulties many people face when it comes to promoting intellectual growth with a spouse. We will then need to evaluate the way some couples respond to these difficulties. In doing this, we may be able to identify some general principles which might be applied to specific situations. In addition, let's examine the relationship between this aspect of the search for intimacy and the sacramental dimension of Christian marriage. This process should provide some hints for actions by individuals and by church communities which might help stimulate intellectual growth in marriage.

One of the main reasons the need for continual intellectual stimulation in their marriages escapes most couples is that having the time and opportunity for intellectual development is rather new. When the average life span was thirty years, as it was in the Middle Ages, or even fifty years, as it was at the turn of the century, most people were involved in satisfying basic needs and had little time to consider intellectual growth. This was especially true for parents in lower classes of society. It is difficult to imagine the working class of a Dickens' novel having the opportunity to engage in adult education courses. And even in those levels of society where intellectual growth was considered mandatory, the obligation applied only to men. Women were thought to be much too busy caring for children, and they were also presumed unable to exercise the rational thinking needed for intellectual growth.

With longer life spans and a technology which has decreased the time needed simply to support life, there has been a swelling of interest in education. In the United States not only do all children under age sixteen attend school, but there has been a tremendous increase in college education as well. As the amount of leisure time has grown, many people have turned to adult education after the completion of formal schooling. In short, in modern technological societies, opportunities for intellectual growth are available to a majority of members, while in the past they were reserved for those who were able to hire others to care for their basic needs.

Unfortunately, this phenomenon of increased leisure time for large numbers of people, as well as longer life spans and smaller families, has not been accompanied by widespread understanding of how to use these opportunities for the betterment of individuals and societies. The quality of television programming reveals that growth in the intellectual dimension of the human personality is not a high priority among those responsible for the media. Intellectual growth beyond that required for success in a career is just beginning to receive attention as an asset for people preparing for full lives in their later years. Lifecycle theories show that we need different intellectual tools during our retirement years than we need when we are just beginning as parents and professionals.

A second, and possibly more difficult, problem is tied to the male-female role stereotypes which prevailed in previous generations. Not only the stereotype which holds women to be less capable of rational thought, but also the myth of male superiority, has created a situation where it is extremely difficult to look upon marriage as the place to give or receive intellectual stimulation. From the ancients we learned that a man should seek one woman as a mistress for sexual pleasure, another as a wife to mother his children, and a third person (most often another male) to be a friend and intellectual companion. Even the churches and others who eventually counseled combining the mistress and wife roles seldom considered the wife as a potential intellectual companion. It would not do for the woman, who was to be subject to her husband, to be his intellectual equal. This attitude is hardly conducive to marital relationships in which a woman will feel free to challenge her husband to develop his intellectual skills or in which a husband will think it important to encourage his wife in the same area.

With so few role models available, it is little wonder that many couples encounter tension in this area of their married lives. In many instances couples will not even consider their failure to grow in wisdom as a possible cause of the problems they are experiencing in their marriage. For example, one man, a college graduate and successful businessman, seems to take great delight in proclaiming, "I never read a book." His wife, who did not complete college, is known to be an avid reader, but they never discuss what she reads. Whenever she engages in an activity requiring her considerable intellectual skills, she can be sure she will receive no encouragement from him. After fifteen years of marriage, she excuses his behavior by saying, "He's so busy he doesn't have time to notice." Yet, she is quite hurt by his lack of interst, and it is obvious that they do not communicate well in other areas. Both of them are caught by the social mythology which says that in order to be head of the family a man must be more intelligent. A wife, therefore, should not strive to acquire as much knowledge as her husband possesses. They have not been able to confront the fallacy of this model, probably because they lack good communication skills; but another reason is their unfamiliarity with couples who have managed the problems of individual intellectual growth in marriage.

This example demonstrates the need for role models who are willing to admit that the search for intellectual intimacy in marriage is hard work, but also rewarding. We need couples who are willing to share their stories of how they have confronted the stereotypes, moved beyond them to grow intellectually, and increased the degree of intimacy in their relationships. It is not enough to have feature stories on successful business persons and artists who have combined marriage and career. We need to examine the lives of couples who are quietly seeking intimacy and who, in the process, have discovered that developing the intellectual dimension of their lives has enriched their experience.

At the present time, couples who are experimenting with new approaches to growth in marriage have not always consciously identified the need for intellectual growth. From my observation, it seems that many of these couples discover instead the stimulation and support of this dimension of their relationship as a by-product of their commitment to continue to find ways to keep their love growing. If we examine what these people have done, we should find some hints which would be applicable in other marriages.

For example, a couple in California is quite interested in religious education. The wife would like to become a director of religious education in a parish. The husband retired from the business world at age fifty and does small carpentry jobs to supplement their income. His more pressing interest, however, is in biblical studies. Both of them have entered a graduate program in religious studies. Despite the demands of the program and the fact that neither of them has a bachelor's degree, they are very happy in their role as students. Obviously, this did not just happen to them overnight. Much planning went into their decision. The search for intimacy, which is part of their marital relationship, led them to discover that there are new dimensions to life which they had not considered when the children were small and work was demanding.

For another couple, the move into areas of growth in learning came after time spent in all the various leisure activities available to upper-middle-class suburban people. Vacations, golf, tennis, parties, summer home, large family, and successful business are still part of their life, but they have gradually come to recognize the need to move beyond these interests. She has entered a scholar's program at the local university, and he has enrolled in a gourmet cooking course. To the delight of his family and friends, he is busily practicing his newly acquired cooking skills, something he would never have learned in a traditional career-centered educational program of his college years. When she attended college, women did not seriously prepare for graduate level courses. Now, if she should want to enter a professional program when her children are older, she will have the necessary background. Though their growth interests are in different areas, they are benefiting from each other's newly developed talents. She enjoys his cooking, and he is acquiring knowledge in discussions about her course work.

Development of the intellectual dimension of life does not always mean formal courses in a university program. As our gourmet cook demonstrates, developing an expertise in a new area helps us appreciate the fullness of life. Sometimes we have lost our enthusiasm for a skill because we have practiced it for so long. The husband has come to realize that his wife, who has mastered the important task of home-making, would be stimulated in a formal program. She, in turn, recognizes his need to move into an entirely new interest. Others find less formal ways of expanding their knowledge, but still discover that lifelong learning is an important ingredient of happier, longer lives.

There is no *one* way to have a successful marriage or no particular formula which will assure the proper way to intellectual growth and development; but as I analyzed the above examples and considered other instances where couples appear to be dealing with this dimension of their married life, I find some general principles which seem to have been followed. These principles suggest questions that a couple could consider when they want to know if they have recognized their need for growth and development.

First of all, *intimacy in marriage requires constant renewal of commitment by both partners.* When was the last time you and your spouse had a serious talk about your growth and development in intimacy? Have you ever thought about the examples of married life which the two of you brought to your marriage from the marriages of your parents? How often do you react to your spouse's behavior because it is not what *you* had expected of him or her? What role models are acknowledged to exist in your marriage? How would you react to your partner's interest in changing role expectations? Are you both willing to face the fact that you have changed since your wedding?

Secondly, *the best way to grow in intimacy is to be satisfied with your own development and to be free to allow your spouse the oppor-*

tunity to pursue areas that are not of interest to you. Do you react in a jealous manner to your spouse's outside interests? When was the last time you seriously considered your situation in life with an eye to evaluation and possible change? Are you happy with the thought that your spouse might be doing something other than what you had expected of a husband or wife? Are you willing to make whatever lifestyle changes are necessary to enable your spouse to pursue a new interest?

Third, *at different stages of a person's life he or she will discover interests which require new knowledge or skills.* Are you or your spouse bored with your present leisure-time activities? When was the last time you tried something new? Have either of you considered a change in career? Have you ever discussed the fact that your interests have changed? Does the wife recognize that her husband's work is not *always* exciting? Does the husband acknowledge that as the children grow older, his wife needs to spend less time on child-related activities? Do you ever talk about what you might do when you retire? What plans are you making for what you might do then? How do you respond to changes in the world around you?

Lastly, *never use your intellectual development as a means of avoiding involvement with your marriage partner.* If you decide to return to school or pursue a new interst, will this mean you have no time to be involved in activities with your spouse? Do you see your intellectual pursuits as a way of getting even with or showing up your spouse? Do you find yourself looking down on your spouse because that person does not share a particular intellectual interest of yours? What are you doing to encourage your spouse to continually grow and develop?

With these general principles in mind, a couple can evaluate their marriage and consider whether they have faced the fact that marriage in a modern technological society demands that the partners be aware of the continuing process of growth and development which contributes to maturity and happiness. They can also examine the amount of attention they have paid to the need to encourage each other in the intellectual dimension of personality growth. Though there are no pat formulas for how to grow in wisdom, a couple should begin to work out their own answers to the challenge.

The search for intimacy in marriage requires that a couple be aware of the barriers to achieving this intimacy. They must, if they hope to maintain a marriage that is open to growth and development, be open to various ways they can assist the process. Heavy emphasis on the physical aspects of sexual intimacy often ignores the fact that couples do not spend their entire married life in bed. A man and woman who hope to continue to relate to each other as mature human beings during the various "passages" of married life must recognize the importance of lifelong learning.

The search for intimacy in Christian marriage is particularly important. Only when partners are constantly perfecting their ability to grow in intimacy, while at the same time allowing each other to grow as individuals, will they be able to sustain a lifelong union that will "somehow reflect the union of Christ and the Church" (Eph 5:32). In short, marriage for couples who live until they are both past the age of seventy requires that the partners acquire new knowledge and skills through the years. A sacramental marriage in which the couple grows in wisdom and grace will reflect to the community the kind of love commitment that is somewhat similar to the love commitment of Yahweh to Israel and Christ to the Church. Christians who marry have a responsibility to sustain this capacity in their marriage. Pursuit of self-knowledge, as well as knowledge of the world in which we live, is an excellent way to assure that the marriage does not grow dull and routine. If that should happen, it would be difficult for anyone, including the couple, to recognize the love commitment of a living God.

Yet as we observed, it is difficult for most couples to act on the idea of the need for continual intellectual growth. It is in this area that church communities can be of assistance. Parish activities should be initiated that will excite couples about the prospects of the search for intimacy contributing to the sacramental character of marriage. Couples should be encouraged to talk about their experience of marriage to inform theologians and church leaders about the mystery of Christ and the Church. Adult education programs should be designed that will entice people away from television and broaden their perspective on life.

There is no easy way to bury the myths that we have examined and which are the roots of many problems we encounter as we seek to grow in our marriage relationships. Neither are the examples we examined perfect patterns to assure success in marriage. And the principles we outlined are merely guidelines to assist couples so their search for intimacy eventually might more fully reveal the mystery of God. The certainty which motivates any attempt to grow in intimacy should be that there is unlimited grace waiting to be tapped in the experience of marriage. Unless Christians are willing to tap it, it is possible that our time will lose the revelation of God which is present in the marriage relationship. The entire Church community must work to avoid a loss of that magnitude.

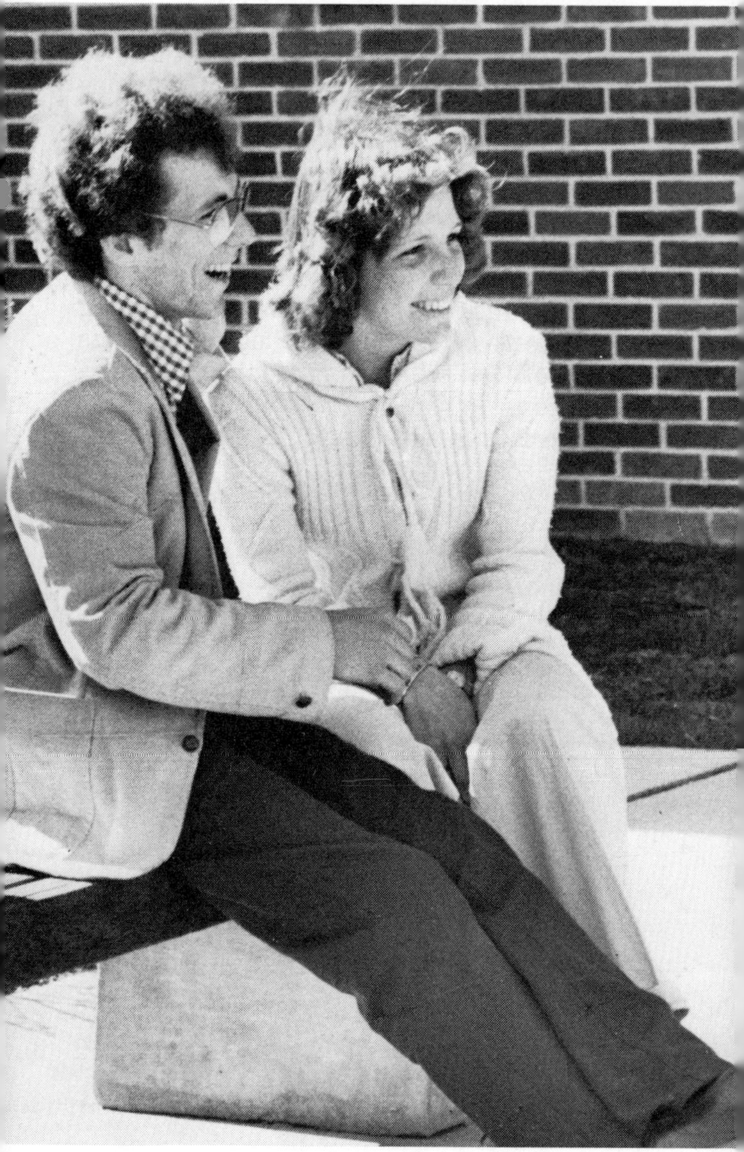

III
Emotional Growth in Marriage
Ken and Becky Eggeman

Ken and Becky Eggeman are educators and trainers in Marriage and Family Development. Ken, who holds a Ph.D. from the University of Nebraska, is Community Services Director for Southern Hills Mental Health Center in Indiana. Becky has her B.S.W. from the University of Evansville and is presently completing advanced work in psychiatric social work at Kent School of Social Work in Louisville, KY.

Victim: *Why do you hold me back? Why won't you let me give? Why do you tie me up every time I get close to expressing myself fully? I feel so uptight I could scream! But you won't even let me do that! The sounds stick in my throat. All I feel is the terrible tightness in my throat, the tension in my shoulders, the knot in my stomach! You are almost incapacitating me! Why do you do these things to me?*

Controller: *Because that way I have you under control. You won't get out of hand and get into something you can't handle! That way you are safe! And you like it that way, too!*

Victim: *I do not! I want out! I want to be free! I want to express myself! I want to let myself go.*

The above quote is a paraphrase from a book, *I Can Only Touch You Now* by Ronald B. Levy. The quote is a rather accurate example of a struggle that exists in each of us individually, and also within our marital relationships.

This dilemma did not come to us out of nowhere. For most of us, as little boys and girls, were taught to suppress, hide, or not share our feelings. Many times the teaching dictate was presented to us as though we had no right to cry, to be angry, or to even feel at all.

Hugh Prather, a contemporary poet, has offered some profound advice in regard to the sharing of feelings. In one of his publications entitled *Notes to Myself,* Prather makes two comments about feelings which are extremely valuable. Prather is responding to the statement, "You shouldn't feel that way."

1. My emotions do not originate in compliance with the laws of Aristotelian logic. My mind cannot know what my body "ought" to be feeling. My body has every reason of its own to be feeling the way it does, and all things being considered (which we cannot do), it couldn't be feeling any other way.

2. Both my body and my emotions were given to me, and it is as futile for me to condemn myself for feeling scared, insecure, or revengeful, as it is for me to get mad at myself for the size of my feet. I am not responsible for my feelings, but for what I do with them.

It is important for us to realize that feelings simply are! They are and they will always be. Understanding and accepting this fact provides the beginning for phenomenal growth in a marital relationship. Growth needs also to take into account the last statement made by Prather where he indicates that we are not responsible for our feelings, but for what we do with them. When two people in an intimate relationship can live out these two realities, "only the best is yet to come!"

One effect of our culture and its norms is that we have become more "thought centered" than "feeling centered." We are more inclined to accept thoughts—sometimes even disagreeable ones—rather than feelings. Perhaps many of us do not understand our feelings or our emotional nature because we have confused thoughts and feelings.

Thoughts come directly from our head, and when we deliver thought messages, they involve several or many words. Usually, thoughts come after some period of contemplation. Although the amount of time may vary, the essential point is that there is a time lapse between when we are stimulated and when we respond. Thoughts are expressed in words and, for so many of us, the words "I feel that" really mean "I think that," creating confusion. For example, "I feel that you are going to be late for dinner" is a thought, not a feeling. To express it as a feeling is to distort its message.

Feelings, on the other hand, come from the "gut" rather than the "head." In almost all situations, feelings can be expressed through one word, namely: I am "sad," "glad," "angry," "happy," "hurt," or "excited." Feelings come immediately and do not entail reflection over a period of time. Frequently, feelings are expressed nonverbally (headaches, red cheeks, sweaty palms, smiles, tears, jumping up and down, etc.). Again, if you are using words "I feel that," chances are you are sharing a thought, not a feeling.

Most research has indicated that substantially over half of the messages sent through our communication efforts involve the emotional or feeling dimension. Moreover, many psychologists and mental health professionals suggest that in our efforts to understand each other we deal only with words which may amount to less than ten percent of our messages.

Virginia Satir, a renowned family specialist, indicates that much of our message in communication is never shared. The result is that the recipient of the message, "makes it up." Making assumptions about what our mate is communicating is dangerous. If, according to the experts, we are only communicating ten percent of our messages, then there is a whole area, ninety percent of potential understanding, we are overlooking in our marital communication.

Discovery and enrichment on the emotional level of communication in a marital relationship are significantly stressed in many communication weekends. The leaders of these events do their best to help couples work at sharing feelings. Some very important concepts are emphasized in marital growth related to feelings:

1. All our feelings are OK. What we do about them may create problems for us and others, but the feelings still remain OK.

Feelings are a sign of health, not a sign of sickness.

2. Feelings are not permanent; they are changeable and movable. This applies to positive as well as negative feelings. This means that positive feelings can be lost, and negative feelings can be changed into positive feelings. Just because someone is happy does not guarantee eternal happiness; and just because someone is angry does not suggest that the person will be angry forever.

Dealing with feelings in a couple relationship is crucial to the success of a good, intimate, growing, and supportive marriage. There are two primary ways in which we choose not to deal with our emotional vibrations and share feelings. One way is to ignore our feelings and tell ourselves: "Yes, I have 'the feeling,' but I don't want to do anything about it." We can hold our stomachs or our heads in pain, yet not say, "I'm hurt" or "I'm angry." We do not express our needs to our mate, obviously ignoring our feelings.

The second way we choose not to deal with feelings is to deny that we have them. A good example of this type of denial is to rub our head in obvious pain, yet say, "No, I don't have any pain. No, I'm not angry or upset." A pertinent example would be men experiencing sadness: they don't cry because they may be seen as weak or insecure. Some men can have tears in their eyes and faces puffed up with pain, yet they respond and say, "No, I'm not upset. I'm a man. I can handle anything."

Ignoring and denying feelings is a primary cause of stress and problems in marriage as well as an example of dishonesty and lack of trust in couple communication. If feelings are not expressed directly and openly, it is certain that they will come out indirectly and be expressed nonverbally. What can we expect then in the marital relationship? The answer is simple, yet frightening—trouble.

Many of us attempt to act on our feelings. Sometimes we act appropriately, and other times inappropriately. Acting on feelings inappropriately can be almost as dangerous as ignoring or denying that we have feelings. Some of the common ways of inappropriate acting are: Blaming, Attacking, Taking Flight, Rationalizing, and some uses of We/They.

Blaming—"You make me angry when you call me names." This is inappropriate because no other person makes us angry. We get angry ourselves. The behavior of our mate may cause us problems, and we react in anger. Blaming is an invitation to fight. "You made me feel bad, so I'll make you feel bad." This is a trap that we so easily fall into in marriage. A better response in this situation would be: "I'm angry because I feel put down when you call me names." No blame; just a statement of fact.

Attacking—"I wish you'd clean up your act. I'm wondering if you treat everybody like that." Attacking our mate is sending the message that we're out to prove he or she has got things messed up. A better response might be to share our feeling and state our need: "I feel (state the feeling), and I need you to change your behavior."

Taking Flight—In situations where we choose not to act on our feelings, we are probably just copping out. Reading the newspaper at mealtime, watching television, or cleaning the house to escape our mate—all of these activities can be appropriate, but they become inappropriate when we choose to do them rather than work through our feelings.

Rationalizing—"Oh, that's me. You know I'm just sensitive." "I've had a hard day, and I don't want to talk about it." "If we only had more time, we could work through these things better." It is easy to find an excuse for anything. All of us would be wealthy if we were paid for our excuses.

We/They—Many times in place of "I" we use "We." This is over-responsibility. It is inappropriate to say "We" when we really mean "I." Under-responsibility is saying "They" when we mean "I." So often in sharing our feelings, we think that "We" or "They" may be more palatable for our mate. In doing so, we are sending a very confused message. "We really got upset with you at the party last night." "They really got upset with you at the party last night." Rather, "I really got upset with your behavior at the party last night."

Emotional Growth and Stability

There are three steps necessary to maintain and preserve emotional growth and stability in ourselves and in our marriages:

Step #1: We need to recognize that we have emotions and will always have emotions. By this recognition, we are also saying that our mate has emotions and will always have emotions.

Step #2: We need to accept our feelings. Feelings are, and they are OK. "I am angry, and that is OK." "My mate is angry, and that is OK."

Step #3: We need to share our feelings and act appropriately. We need to speak from our "self" and use "I" in our sharing. In so doing, we will assume responsibility for our feelings and avoid the problems caused by blaming, attacking, taking flight, rationalizing, and using we/they.

What can we expect from our marriages in response to following these three steps? When we recognize, accept, and appropriately share our feelings, our mate is given the space and opportunity to care for us. Our mate does not have to be concerned about defending himself or herself but can focus on attending, loving, and caring. We all need the right environment to effectively love and care, and this process of sharing our feelings naturally provides such a setting.

A second result is that a clear form of communication is established. The chances of a pattern of communication yielding growth and satisfaction are much higher when we are not confused by mixed and distorted messages. What Virginia Satir has suggested must be emphasized once more—if we are in the midst of unclear message-sending we "make things up," creating trouble for ourselves and those we love.

A third result is that we have set the stage for affirmation. When we can affirm our spouses, we are truly in a caring and loving relationship. When we can say, "I affirm you," we are saying, "I believe you are special!"

There are important cautions and guidelines to be considered when we share our feelings. In sharing feelings, it is important to be sensitive to your mate in light of his/her ability to receive your feelings. Learning about your mate's ability to receive your feelings may take time and practice. Remember that the result may be less rewarding when your spouse is not ready and prepared to receive your feelings.

There is an appropriate time and place to share feelings with your mate. Sharing your anger about your spouse's appearance while at the bridge table is highly inappropriate. Or, sharing your happiness regarding your day's work is inappropriate when your mate is depressed about his or her work day. Learning about time and place will take time and practice. The important thing to remember is: try not to get discouraged about your mistakes.

Understanding the risk that you take in sharing your feelings is crucial. Sharing your feelings is a statement of fact when there is no blaming, attacking, or rationalizing. The risk is that your mate may choose to ignore, deny, or not respond to your sharing. Don't give up! Keep in mind that sharing feelings is not a demand made on your mate—it is simply a request to be attended to and cared for.

Emotional growth? Yes, for most of us this is our biggest area of unrealized potential. A case of support for marital growth is presented in *The Handbook of the Association of Couples for Marriage Enrichment* (ACME), part of which is appropriate here:

> Hardly anyone, until recently, has recognized getting married for what it really is—the embarking of two people on an exceedingly difficult and complicated enterprise capable of bringing the deep and abiding satisfaction of a shared life, but yielding its rewards only to those who will work for them with clear insight and sustained effort. Albert Einstein once said that most people go through life and never develop more than ten percent of their intellectual potential. He might equally well have said that most married couples never develop more than ten percent of their marital potential.

Let's all become more aware of the potential that lies within our own marriage. Start by sharing a feeling!

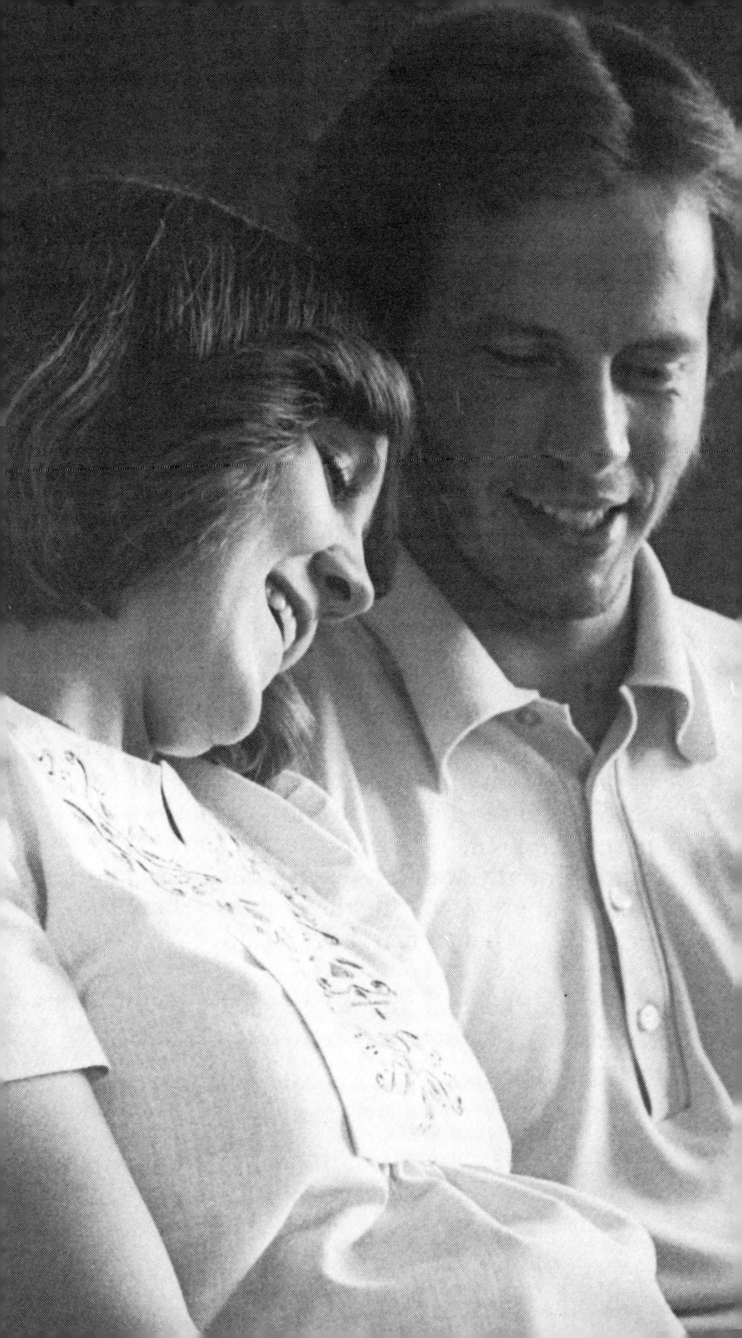

IV
Spiritual Growth in Marriage

Fr. Gordon Lester, C.SS.R.

Father Gordon Lester is Director of Picture Rocks Retreat in Arizona. He was formerly the director of the Family Life Office for the Diocese of Spokane, WA. He is the author of When Love Seeks New Depths, *a book of reflections on married life, published by Abbey Press.*

Marriage is often looked upon as a matter of gutsy survival. The truth is it is both a challenge and a stimulus to spiritual growth. This notion is so unpublicized that it cannot even be called unpopular. It is, in fact, largely unrecognized, even unsuspected.

There are items in abundance which help to create the void of realization that marriage has a spiritual dimension at all.

Item Marriage preparation has too long been limited to a blustery or insipid review of church rules to be kept. Marriage as a sacrament is too often mentioned as hardly more than a well-worn label indicating a bagful of graces for keeping the rules.

Item Love is too often regarded as a feeling which mysteriously comes over a person and just as mysteriously disappears, leaving marriage as no more than a rugged battle to hang in there and hope.

Item Many discover that getting married was a desperate flight to intimacy and being married becomes a burdensome pressure to escape to aloneness and freedom.

Item Perhaps, the truest statement of modern youth is that a piece of paper does not make a marriage. The trouble is that living together does not make a marriage either.

Item For my own church, "that does not make mistakes," it is hard to understand the quirk of history which led that church to decide on the juridical essence of marriage seven centuries before it began to search for the theological meaning of marriage.

Item A lot of good, solid married couples have a healthy contempt for what priests tell them about marriage. A lot of good, solid married couples are crying silently to hear in church something real and nourishing and inspirational about marriage.

Item A major trouble with marriage is that it begins in a glow of love without awareness that the sense of love keeps shifting, and two people married to each other have to keep searching and meeting in love's new direction.

Item People are generally scared stiff, no matter what their brave front, to expose their marriage to an atmosphere of spiritual growth like a retreat or to any tampering by "experts" like counsellors or enrichment teams.

Item The result is that married couples look for help only when they reach a point of desperation. By that time, they are two individuals looking for a sky-hook, rather than a couple looking for growth.

The focus of my attention will be to set aside the negatives and to share something of the spiritual potential which has been discovered and begun to be realized by so many couples in retreats and other enrichment programs. The spiritual is not a venture into the unreal. Rather, the spiritual is the deepest human reality.

Most people suspect that the spiritual has something to do with God. Yet, entering the spiritual means for many entering the unknown, and that is scary for all but the most audacious and adventurous.

And the way the label "spiritual" is misused does not help. Some misuse it by saying that being spiritual means having no interest in anything so fleshy as sex. Others nurse the notion that being spiritual means having a strong attraction to and feeling for churchy things. Some of the most spiritual people I have known are unmistakably erotic and unequivocally unchurched.

Actually, being spiritual merely means being a whole human being with chief attention on the most important part of humanness, the deepest reality of humanness. Sex just may be the best example of what I mean. Sex, as a fleshy pursuit, eventually becomes jaded and boring, more desperate or compulsive than fulfilling. Sex as a passionate expression of a deep and committed personal relationship is alive and creative, always new and fresh, reaching far beyond two bodies in contact. The difference between the two is the inclusion or exclusion of the human spirit.

Using sex in comparison with the spiritual is no whim, nor is it capricious. Sex involves the whole person—from the body to the spirit. The spiritual involves the whole person—from the spirit to the body. Marriage is a union of persons—not just of bodies or ideas or feelings or economic effort or any isolated part of being human or living human life.

To grow spiritually one needs to reflect. To reflect, one bends back mentally to reexamine experience, to search for the thread of meaning, linking the past to the present moment, to draw out the value, to line up the direction one wants to take, to shuck off the diversions obstructing the goal. For this kind of reflection, one needs alone-time, often away-time.

A married couple's retreat, an enrichment program, an Encounter are all intended to give a review from a new vantage point, a new vision into the future. Some programs have a director and content of priceless value. Others, unfortunately, have little value and can turn people off for years, or forever. Spiritual directors should be sought out as carefully as brain surgeons or ob-gyn specialists. The preciousness of what is concerned makes the care in selection obvious.

One problem is that too many programs geared for married life focus only on sociological or psychological aspects. They miss or ignore the spiritual dimension. Christ hardly enters in, if at all.

When we speak of Christian marriage as a sacrament, we are not talking about an extra, added attraction. We are talking about the heart of what Christian marriage is. Only by being what it is meant to be can marriage realize its human potential, not to mention its Christian potential.

When we speak of Christian marriage, we

are not speaking about a denominational ceremony. We are speaking about a human reality redeemed and given a new meaning by Christ. When we speak about any redeemed human reality, we recognize that all things human need Christ's redemption in order to be what they are supposed to be in the plan, or in the reality of God.

The trouble is that marriage has been recognized by all tribes and peoples through history as utterly human, even if suspected of being somewhat sacred. Even in the centuries of Christianity, marriage, until recently, was locked into human custom. Only in the most recent times has marriage come to be regarded as no longer an unavoidable economic necessity. It is not a status achievement for social acceptance. It is not an exclusive outlet for sex or a mere production system supplying the world's demand for human beings. All these primitive needs have had a great influence in suppressing what Christ and Paul were talking about when they spoke of marriage. The spirituality of marriage has just begun to come into being in the attention of the Church, although it has long been realized in the living experience of many called to the vocation of marriage.

To be told what to do to enrich a marriage helps only up to a point. Far more fruitful is to look within oneself and one's experiences for new depth and meaning. Here a married couples' retreat offers the greatest promise.

Retreats emphasize reflection—in the presence of God. Workshops (enrichments, encounters) emphasize verbalization and sharing—in the presence of fellow pilgrims. Reflection is something of a search into a mystery: a bottomless depth. Verbalization expresses what is known, but also reflects what is not known: built-in limitations. Sharing involves a decision or a caution on how far or how deep one thinks it wise to open up. Retreat reflection offers the comfort and security that God will understand inner thoughts if no one else does.

Spirituality is primarily living in the awareness of God's presence. Making a retreat is a matter of going to the Source of enlightenment and strength. It is more a search for God within the experience of one's own marriage and family than comparing notes with the marriage and family of others. Still, the choice depends on where one is and what one needs—now. Most important is that every marriage and family needs attention. Not just attention to daily demands, but attention in depth reflection, full and undivided, at regular intervals.

But let me work my way back to the same point from a different direction.

There are marriage programs geared to repair the broken-down marriage, and there are programs aimed at bolstering the sagging marriage. There are also programs which claim to make the good marriage perfect. In fact, so much attention has been put on the marital health quotient that it's too often like reading the symptoms of a mental disorder or some exotic venereal disease in *Reader's Digest* and having a self-diagnosis of guilt or infection looming like an avenging angel appearing suddenly in the sky.

What about the normal marriage? What

about your marriage?

The most normal thing about any marriage is that it is unique and personal. Marriage is a union of two human beings: one man, one woman. Just as a person grows with age and experience, so this intimate union of persons grows with age and experience. The chief problem of life, perhaps, is that both the person and the marriage are inclined to get hooked at a certain level of growth. If both the man and the woman get hooked at the same level, there may not be much of a problem because there is no change in the problem. What seems far more common or normal is that husband and wife mature to different levels at a different pace.

There is no question about the value of developing communication techniques and skills. But it is not an ultimate value. There must be something to communicate which the other is interested in receiving. If you want to listen to puerile conversations, listen to groups exchanging their feeling reactions to insignificant life happenings. It's about as gripping as people exchanging their blood pressure readings.

Nor can good marriage communication be built on analysis of the stock market, the baseball standings, the political windcurrents, the cause for social justice, or the fashion trends.

Marriage, really, is the communication of the total person—ideas, feelings, experience, hopes, dreams, fantasies, plans, reactions to the realities of life—as life touches the person in depth. If a person has closed off all the avenues of inner growth or allowed self to be frozen at a certain level of maturity, communication becomes as boring and predictable as a cracked record. Person-communication has to get into one's sense of the meaning of life, the values in conflict, the purpose, the goals. This calls for spiritual search and for spiritual listening.

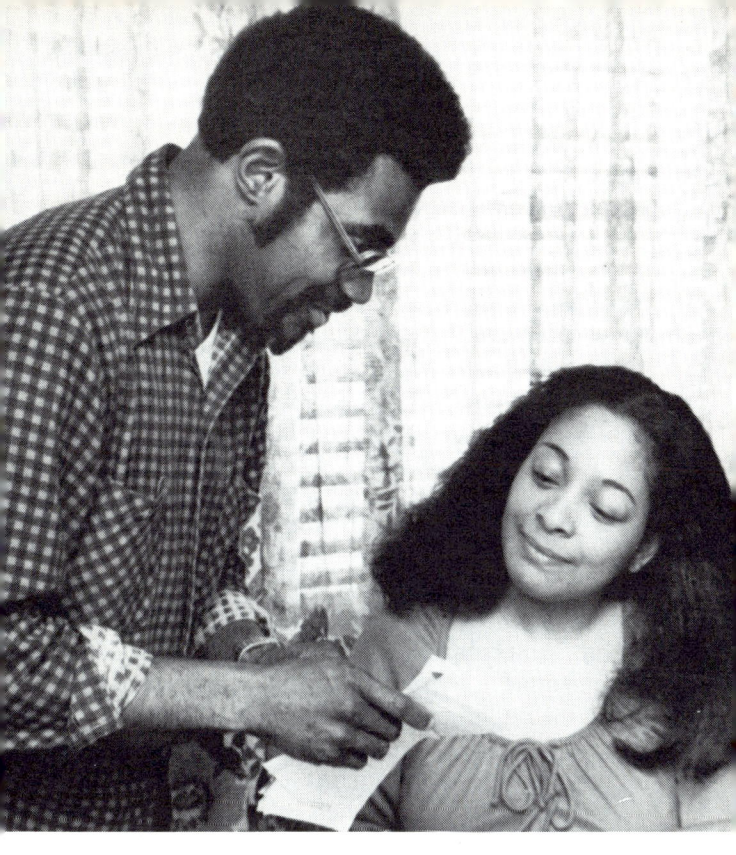

Persons are inclined to grow at least in response to the experience of life. They may grow into a hard shell, or they may blossom into rare wisdom and beauty. The same thing happens to the union of persons we call marriage. It either atrophies or bears fruit. Spiritual reflection is what makes the difference.

The genius of a live marriage is that a man helps a woman grow as a person, a woman helps a man grow as a person. Both personal blind spots and male-female blind spots are compensated for by one who sees from a different vantage point, by one who loves and listens to the one with blind spots. In marriage, there is the potential of two visions of the truth and two senses of the good. There can be the healing of touch where words bruise or confuse, the warmth of affection to soften the sharpness of the mind, the loving and the being loved, and the finding of oneself in the other. This is sharing of spiritual depth.

Let's reflect further on this. Every person—at some time of life—becomes lost, confused, unexplainable, groping and desperate for a sense of worth and meaning. Talk that denies this is most often bravado or escape from facing reality, maybe even blindness to facts, or just a sign that the person talking does not trust his or her intimate self to the other person. Because of the other's failure to understand or tendency to twist one's meaning to make it acceptable, breakdown of trust happens in marriage and distorts the union of persons into a painful or uncomfortable or retarding pair of roommates.

How does marriage avoid or move beyond such pitfalls and breakdowns? Basically, by coming to realize or by remembering that the relationship of marriage is a visible, tangible, human expression of the relationship between God and human beings, especially the faithful. On the one hand, married fidelity is called to be like God's fidelity. On the other hand, a husband and wife's striving to become "two in one flesh" is fraught with as many missteps as human beings seeking union with God. So we are back to spiritual reflection in pursuit of a mystery, not dead-ended by an impossible problem.

This may sound like a quick turn of a corner or a bit much for anyone resigned to a purely secular world. Don't, however, reject this as religious fanaticism, or as the kind of faith which is not more than a comfortable concoction of the mind to deaden the sting of real life.

The true faith deals with facts, facts that are beyond the immediate perception of the mind, but which are nontheless real. Marriage has for too long been regarded and dealt with as a mere human phenomenon, modified only by anthropological variations. Even natural marriage is a sign of underlying spiritual realities.

By reality, as known by faith, we have long accepted that marriage is a sacrament. We have lately come to realize that for this sacrament to be understood and to be fully appreciated couples must discover and develop awareness of the presence of God in the human reality of marriage. The mystery of marriage (as accented by so many programs) is not how a man and a woman can live happily together for life. The mystery of marriage is how God uniquely expresses himself both in its daily life and in its hidden depths. The mystery of marriage is how couples can and do discover God through each other, express his presence to each other, and become to others a visible sign of the mystery of God himself.

This is why I think married couples' retreats are of irreplaceable importance. Retreats, at least potentially, give a couple the atmosphere and the mood to search into their experience and to find the presence of God in their life together. Retreats help to discover the authentic spirituality that belongs to the vocation of marriage and to avoid diversion into another spirituality designed for or flowing from another way of life, that is, celibacy. For far too long, unsuitable spiritualities have been imposed on marriage and have acted as divisive forces in marriage, which God designed as a way to come to each other and to him through each other.

If we find in Scripture that life is an expression of God's love for us and a record of human response to his invitation to love him, we have found the underlying heart of marriage as a prophetic sign. God may be a pure spirit, but as a pure spirit he has chosen to communicate himself to us most clearly and most frequently in human terms. So we look to human reality, and specifically to the human reality of marriage, not as a self-explanatory dead end, but rather as a revelation of God himself. Looking for God in marriage, or any place else in human reality, is not an easy or quickly finished process. It does not happen once and for all. It is as twisting and turning as life itself. It is moving with life as it is, never capturing life and holding it in a firm grip as we are tempted to want it to be. It calls for going back to the mountain to pray over and over again, as Christ himself kept doing in his lifetime.

Many roads can be taken through Scripture to find the way through marriage to God. I have my route. You, no doubt, have yours. But outlining the route is another story for another time. Meanwhile, God has his own way of making himself known and felt. The first move is to want him to make contact—then listen! That is spiritual reflection. That is prayer.

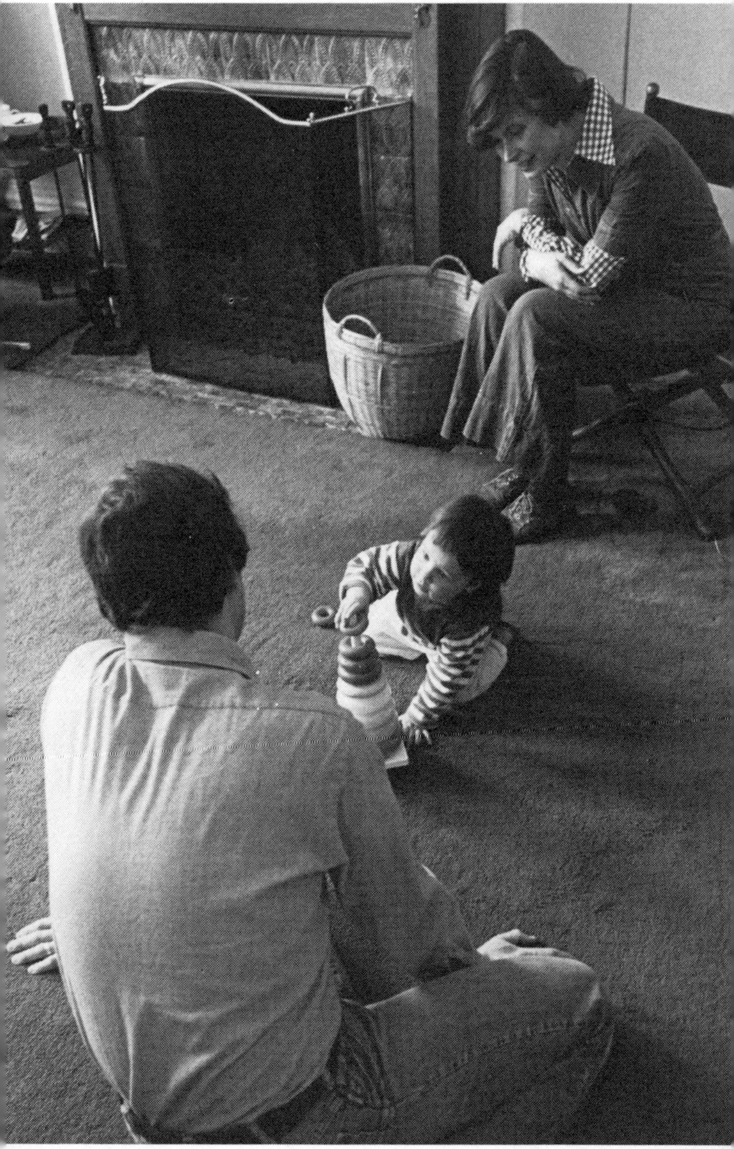

V
Parenting and Marital Love: When Is It Good Enough?

Arthur Mandelbaum

Arthur Mandelbaum, M.S.W. is the director of the Marriage and Family Program of the Menninger Foundation, Topeka, KS. A member of the American Group Psychotherapy Association, Mr. Mandelbaum has had over forty articles published in professional journals. He is married and the father of one.

I have been quite astonished lately to observe how frightened spouses are by the responsibilities of marriage and parenting. This has led me to seriously consider urging moderation in this area. Even in the all important task of being a spouse and being a parent, we all need a sense of "well enough" in addition to a vision of the unattainable ideal. A sense of moderation with regard to these responsibilities in the family would allow space and time for development to unfold, and for spontaneity, joy, and adaptability to be experienced in these intimate human relationships. It would make it possible to assume the tasks and responsibilities of these roles, without their being seen as so monumentally difficult that they paralyze people.

Among committed idealists, the responsibilities of being a spouse and a parent are taken on with such high expectations and seriousness that enjoyment of marital life is greatly diminished. Responsibilities weigh so heavily on the couple that spontaneity is lost, and ways of doing things become rigid and confining for each family member.

It is astonishing, but not a complete surprise, to see how many spouses are frightened of their marital partners, and how parents are so frightened of their children that their good, intelligent, and sensitive common sense vanishes in everyday living. When seen in clinics, these parents view themselves as helpless and inept, and often appeal to their children to assume parental responsibilities. But when parents abdicate their power, their children become demanding, manipulative tyrants, who eventually become frightened of their own inappropriate strength. These are called parental children, taking over tasks and responsibilities in a confused and frightened way. They can then pay very little attention to their responsibilities at school and to their need to play with their peers and enjoy life at their appropriate age level. Such a psychological burden is too heavy for them to carry so early in life, and they develop a pseudomaturity to deal with their parents.

Many spouses are so oriented by idealism in marriage that they are actually frightened of each other and immobilized by an overwhelming sense of responsibility. Quite the opposite is the approach to marriage which regards it as a light matter entered into by simply falling in love, so that one loses sight of the other spouse as partner in a working relationship. The poet Rilke emphasized the difficulty there was in loving another and called it hard work, noting that since young people are unprepared for such difficulties, society has tried to make marriage into something "easy and frivolous."

Marriage and Striving for Excellence

Rilke went on to describe the ways young people "fling themselves at each other in the impatience and haste of their passion and do not notice at all what a lack of mutual esteem lies in this disordered giving of themselves." With the amazing insight and intuition of the artist, Rilke saw the unjust, overbearing, and intolerant manner of the young unmarried couple toward each other, leading to serious marital conflict and a too easy giving up on the task of working on their relationship. But Rilke underestimated the complexity of the marital relationship, and what is brought to it from the family of origin of young newlyweds.

Separation from their own parents and siblings is one of the chief motives for marriage for some young adults who find no other alternatives for achieving a sense of being free and separate persons. They may then reluctantly but hastily pull away from their parents, with a profound sense of disloyalty and guilt for deserting them. When the husband is caught in this dilemma of separation and is still primarily committed to and even dependent on his parents, the wife can only sense partial and sometimes indifferent commitment to their new and struggling family unit. In turn, the wife also may be struggling with some problems of achieving young adulthood. There is no solitude then for such spouses (solitude in the sense of self as independent and autonomous), since they are intensely attached to their own parents and cannot stand sufficiently apart from them to see and experience their marital partners in an objective way. Their fantasies of what marriage is like clash with what it actually turns out to be.

Couples who can for a time accept the fact of their deep attachments to their families of origin, without letting them compete with their own struggles to love each other in this real world, will be able to experience the growth that they need. Fears of intimacy and of facing the sticky issues and conflicts that intimacy implies can be dealt with without destroying their earlier commitments and loyalties. There is a transfer of old expectations into the marital relationship along with fresh hopes, and this gives them a new chance within their marriage to resolve old conflicts. If assisted by a family of origin, which tempers its demands, the couple can be supported in a new beginning and can enter into new areas of development. Leaving one family system to create another is a formidable task, but it does not have to be done either through anarchy and revolution or through hopeless compliance and depression.

It is the rare individual who enters marriage wholly free and separated from his or her family of origin. For one spouse to expect this of the other is an intolerant position. It is good enough for the spouse to continue to pay homage to parents and to siblings and, if fortunate enough to still have them, to grandparents. But homage must be in moderation as an expression of love and caring through dignified acts of respect which do not intrude too deeply into the relationship of the couple. It must also be balanced so that the husband does not fear or envy too much his wife's attachment to her family, and she does not fear too much the husband's devotion to his parents and siblings. Each spouse assists the other to maintain his or her roots but also encourages new perspectives, new goals, fresh starts.

You will note the words "not fear too much." They highlight the fact that in all of us there is some tinge of fear that we will not be able to disengage ourselves from our family of origin, not be able to claim our partner sufficiently, so that old and new dependencies and expectations can be explored and worked on. This fear of the power and influence of the opposite spouse's family is present in everyone. What is feared is that past relationships may be more powerful than the marriage, and thus conflicts around this fear get played out again and again.

CASE EXAMPLE: A couple in their early forties came with the complaint that the husband had escorted a waitress to another city where they had cocktails together. The couple had been married ten years; the wife was shocked at her husband's action, as well as his wish for a separation and a divorce. The husband explained that every Sunday for the past ten years he and his wife had visited her father and mother. This was a ritual which his wife demanded. Several months ago, his wife had been advised by her father to invest in some real estate, and she had doubled her investment in a very short time. She followed, for a time, her father's suggestion not to tell her husband, but finally confessed to him what she had done, expecting praise and satisfaction. Instead, he had gotten furious and left the house, and then the incident had occurred with the other woman. The husband agreed that he was very angry and saw his wife as so attached to her father that there was no commitment to him as husband. He was unaware of his contribution to the marital problem by his too easy and passive acceptance of the relationship between his wife and her father.

Here we see that the wife never separated from her family of origin and allowed that family to play the major role in her life. Her commitment to her husband was rather weak and accompanied by contempt for his passivity, his compliance in the face of his powerful father-in-law. Thus, no boundaries had been developed to separate her family of origin from her marriage, and the husband had gone along with his wife by not challenging her overinvolvement with her parents.

The Good Enough Parents

The marriage that is "making it," that is "good enough," leads to new opportunities for enrichment through the experiences of being parents. The mother concentrates on her relationship to the infant during the first important months, and the father protects that relationship and makes it possible for the mother to unfold her latent sensitivities and to fully experience the drama of that mother-child relationship. This experience of meeting the needs of a helpless infant begins the long process of differentiation. To nurture and care for her child, under the watchful eye and with the help of her "good enough" husband, now a father too, enables the mother to share the possession of the child with her husband. The addition to the family mobilizes new anxieties and new strengths. Every change in life is a loss and a gaining of knowledge and sensibilities. The "good enough" environment supports the normal crises, assisting the role change into parenthood. The boundaries between the roles of wife and mother and of husband and father are more delicately drawn and, if perceived with "good enough" clarity, can be trespassed upon occasionally, whenever it serves the purpose of caring for and further unfolding the character of each family member.

CASE EXAMPLE: A young colleague reported with joy the birth of his firstborn daughter. His face turned solemn, however, as he described how childish he had been when he and his wife brought the baby home. While his wife was in the hospital, he had cleaned and polished their modest home. His wife came into the apartment and, placing the baby on their bed, had changed the wet diaper, allowing it to fall on the floor. Irritated that his wife had not praised him for the work he had done and that the diaper had fallen on the floor, the man used a tone of voice which expressed his annoyance when he picked up the diaper. His wife, tired and anxious, threw him a look of impatience. He went into the living room, and sitting down heavily, suddenly realized that he was already jealous of his child.

This experience brought forth positive and

negative feelings. It gave the young man some insight into the complexity of his emotions, and showed him he could place a brake on his regression without too much pain and guilt. Becoming a parent means an arousal of memories of what it means to be tiny and helpless, of what it meant when brothers and sisters were born, of what it means to discipline aggression, of the necessity for sharing and moving beyond the solitude which protects our selfhood. In that struggle, a new balance must be sought, a balance which protects differentiation and autonomy for each partner.

With the recovery of a sense of objectivity and the acceptance of new boundaries, the definition of roles does not need to become so blurred that it results in confusion, competition, excessive demands for dependency, and clinging on the part of one or both spouses. What is then set in motion is a more easy sharing of parental decisions which subordinates power issues and keeps them under control. If power becomes an aggressive pursuit, children then have no choice but to ally with one parent or the other, using their available energy in bridging parental differences. Such a bridge is locked into a static position, and the bridge cannot lead anywhere, unless the parents deal with their own differences.

The "good enough" parent will seek to define his or her position clearly and appropriately, making it easier for the other parent to do the same. In everyday life, parents do this naturally and are role models for their children. They close the door to their bedroom when making love. They close the door to the bathroom and protect their own privacy. They do not enter their older children's bedrooms without knocking; they respect the privacy of their children. These intuitive signs of respect convey a basic sense of trust in a mutual bond, and free the children to be themselves. Ellen Glascow put it quite nicely years ago, "After all, there is a freedom in not being loved too deeply, in not being thought of too often. Possessive love makes most of the complications and nearly all of the unhappiness in the world." Such possessive love destroys the boundaries of self.

The Good Enough Child

Finally, one comes to the reality of the "good enough" child. Couples who are "good enough" as parents recognize love and caring as important ingredients in human development. Any demand from a parent that a child be more than "good enough" would seem likely to threaten or weaken the reassurance the child gets from his or her environment being reliable and protective. Here again the protection of boundaries is an important parental responsibility that cannot be forfeited.

The protection of such boundaries means that the parent is consistently working on his or her relatedness to the child which confirms differentiation and autonomy. The mother who is excessively jealous of her daughter and the father who is excessively jealous of his son introduce in their relatedness to their children factors still vibrating in their families of origin and in the marriage. The aggressive and ambitious father or mother may override the pace at which a child can go and so cause the child to surrender a sense of competence. The child may lag behind in school and sense that the only way to defeat controlling and too eager parents is to fail.

CASE EXAMPLE: A prominent lawyer worried why his several sons, all of whom were over twenty, could not leave the home and establish their independence from him. He was tired of supporting them and of their failure to attend college. He mentioned their high intelligence several times during the session. He wanted to kick them out of the home, but his wife opposed such a move. In a burst of real feeling, he spoke of his fear of aging, and of his wife's fear that despite his excellent income, he had few financial reserves and was facing retirement with too few resources. When he demurred about bringing his wife or sons into the next interview, he was startled by my reluctance to believe that he really wanted changes and by my assertion that he really liked having his sons near him because they were obedient and loyal sons. He was angry at my comments and challenged by my expressed doubt that he could get his children to the next session. He was determined to show me I was wrong.

The "good enough" parent who is "good enough" in relating to son or daughter can modify the child's recurring inner sense of dependence, in order to help and allow the child to test the reliability and the firmness of his or her parents. Such parents learn to have confidence in their children's strength to put up with their irrational selves and so earn their praise for an ability to negotiate with them.

It is "good enough" when one talks, listens, negotiates. This is the only way to know enough about our children, so that we refresh and renew our faith in growth and maturity. Each good experience, added to others through each year of growth, enriches marital and parental relationships and is a "good enough" foundation to bear the unexpected, the kind and the cruel events which test all of us. Sorrows and joys can then take their proper place in the accumulation of wisdom, tolerance, and knowledge about oneself, about one's spouse, and about one's children.

Questions for Reflection and Discussion

The Fullness of Physical Love
(see pp. 13-25)

1. Where do we get our concepts of sexuality?

2. How does advertising affect us in ways beyond the pushing of a product?

3. How can we restore excitement and vitality to the ordinary encounters we have every day? Or must they always remain "just ordinary"?

4. What do you experience as the religious side of human sexual expression?

5. What is your reaction to the idea of small group support for married couples? How might this assist in creating a more human and Christian expression of sexuality?

Intellectual Growth and Intimacy
(see pp. 27-39)

1. In your own view does intellectual development present more of an opportunity or a threat to the marriage relationship? Why?

2. Looking at your own marriage, chart the major areas of intellectual development in your life. Do the same thing for your marriage partner. How do they compare?

3. What opportunities for intellectual growth are available to you and your spouse? How might pursuit of these opportunities affect intimacy in your marriage?

4. The author believes that intellectual growth is a special problem at this time. Would you agree with her assessment? Why?

Emotional Growth in Marriage
(see pp. 41-51)

1. What do you think about the claim that not sharing our feelings is a form of dishonesty?

2. What happens when we keep our feelings within us? Will they eventually surface? How?

3. What physical reactions might come from concealing emotions?

4. What does the sharing of emotions add

QUESTIONS FOR REFLECTION AND DISCUSSION

to a marriage? Specifically how does it help the quality of the marital relationship?

Spiritual Growth in Marriage
(see pp. 53-65)

1. How does the prospect of a married couples' retreat sound to you? Are there opportunities in your own area?

2. What does spiritual reflection mean to you? What do you see as its value for married life?

3. Father Lester believes that marriage today is more of a gold mine of riches than ever before. Do you agree with this? How might one realisticaly make this judgment?

4. How does Fr. Lester's definition of spirituality square with your own? Where does what he has to say fit or not fit within your own experience?

Parenting and Marital Love
(see pp. 67-78)

1. How can one secure a realistic view of what might be called the reasonable demands of marriage and family life? What about discussing this with your spouse?

2. How important do you view the need to be clear on your continued relationship to your family of origin? How do you get in touch with the psychological carry-over? Can this be an important topic for you to discuss within your own marriage?

3. The author reveals how difficult it is for many spouses and parents to believe that they are really "good enough"; what does this difficulty reveal about our society?

4. What standards do you use to judge whether you are "good enough"? Where did they come from and how satisfied are you with them?

A Review of Pope John Paul II's Book on Christian Marriage

Paul F. Wilczak

When Cardinal Karol Wojtyla of Cracow, Poland, was called to the papacy in October of 1978, a man of unusual capacity came to world attention. He chose the name of John Paul II, a gesture which emphasized his pastoral and spiritual connection with his three predecessors. Both *Time* and *Newsweek* magazines quickly ran cover stories on the new Pope. At a glance it was obvious that he was an unusual man, and a most extraordinary choice for pope. The first non-Italian pontiff since the Reformation, a rugged sportsman, a brilliant and formidable opponent of Marxism within the paradoxically Catholic-Communist state of Poland, he is at home in half a dozen languages and clearly reaches out toward the diverse peoples and cultures which make up our world.

As a person of Polish-American descent, I was proud yet amazed at the news of Cardinal Wojtyla's election. Here was an ecclesiastical figure of great responsibility, authority, and talent, yet also a person who in 1976 had visited my former parish of Saint Stanislaus in Buffalo, New York. At that time he spoke in a free and casual manner with the people at the parish. Among them was my father, a retired factory worker.

The quality of this person, now called John Paul II, which amazes me most is his capacity to meet people at many different levels. A former factory worker himself, he is at home with laborers. An avid outdoorsman, mountain climber, and skier, he can savor the thrill of meeting and surmounting a physical challenge and appreciate the joy of a strenuous life. A lover of music, he experiences a bond which joins him to many other cultured persons. And his pastoral compassion transcends cultural divisions. Yet what I shall here emphasize more than anything else is the fact that this man of many gifts is also a talented theologian. For a pope to be also a gifted theologian is a rare phenomenon.

Americans now have the opportunity to read John Paul II's theological works. One of them, entitled *Love and Responsibility,* concerns the theology of marriage. First published in 1960, the book has been described in the American popular press as an anticipation of Paul VI's encyclical *Humanae Vitae.* This can be said but involves the risk of missing the work's significance. It would be a gross error to categorize Karol Wojtyla's views on marriage as dated, merely conservative, or simply foreshadowing those of Paul VI. I would like to comment on their creative depth and significance. In my attempt to bring his perspective into focus, I shall rely on the 1962 Polish edition of his book published in Cracow. The abbreviation, MO, for the Polish title will be used in parentheses with page numbers after all quotations.

On first reading this book I was very impressed by its thoughtfulness. The author is a very capable philosophical theologian, well trained in phenomenology. His writing presents a fine analysis of the phenomena of human and marital love, but its philosophical weight makes the reading difficult. This book is worth the effort but certainly demands a good deal of work.

There is no way I could do justice to the book's contents in so brief a commentary. Instead I shall go at once to the very center of John Paul II's vision of marital love. When helpful, I shall quote him directly in my own English translation.

What is immediately striking about his book is its primary concern with marital love seen as, in its very nature, springing of necessity from an appreciation of the value of the person. In this clear, objective emphasis, John Paul II, in my opinion, stands within the philosophical tradition established by the eminent Polish phenomenologist, Roman Ingarden. Both sought to convey the authentic nature of the objects they strove to investigate. Consequently, my own remarks will be aimed at what I consider to be the center of the book: the nature of marital love, the affirmation of the value of the person, and membership of person to person in the sacrament of marriage.

The Nature of Marital Love

The nature of marital love is at the very heart of this book. But the Pope's fundamental understanding of that "nature" is what he calls "metaphysical." What he is trying to say is that if we wish to really understand marriage we must come to grips with a more fundamental reality than the feelings and happenings of the moment. It is in fact this deeper reality that makes of marital love a unified experience. And the experience opens the reality to our eyes.

It would be helpful to quote John Paul II at this point. The following is my own free translation of his words: "We have tried to grasp what distinguishes each love and what is so characteristic about what takes place in the love of husband and wife. Love can indeed be recognized in the individuals' pleasurable feelings of attraction, desire, and friendliness. But love does not culminate in individuals but in a relationship between persons. Mutuality is absolutely essential. A change of emphasis from 'me' to 'us' is no less essential to love than the outward movement of self expressed in attraction, desire, and friendliness. Love is not merely an aspiration but far more a meeting and unification of persons. This meeting and growing unification of the individuals takes place with the firm support of their increasing attraction, desire, and friendliness. This individual experience of love enters into and conditions the interpersonal aspect of love. In the end, the love of two persons is always a unique interpersonal synthesis and harmony of pleasurable attraction, desire, and friendliness" (MO, 84).

What impresses me about the Pope's words is their compassionate realism. His "metaphysics" of love is relevant to real people. And speaking as a marriage counselor, I find much that is relevant to my work in his vision. Marriage counseling deals with problems of mutually expressing and growing in pleasurable attraction, desire, and friendliness. What surprises me is that the present Pope was stressing their importance in marriage eighteen years ago. And his views are of particular relevance today with the mushrooming availability and public acceptance of various marital and sexual therapies. A serious weakness in many of the therapies currently on the market is their lack of a fundamental vision of marital love. They tend to substitute techniques for vision rather than correlating them with such a fundamental understanding. This is particularly true in the sex therapies. Consequently, it would be of benefit to reflect on what John Paul II has said on the connection between sex and love.

He concludes the section of his book on marital love with these words: "The understanding of marital love provides the key to the determination of norms for the whole of sexual morality. We cannot avoid the fact that sex deeply involves the reality of persons. And we respond to that fact with a special personal awareness of a need, accepted as normative, that we be in responsible, personal possession of our own self. In consequence, we cannot speak of relating sexually without also meaning relating personally and in a manner which enters the sphere of those demands which we have set up as a law of married love. These are demands flowing from the norm based on what it is to be a person. Thus, marital love alone, although it is in its own nature different from all other forms of love, cannot be shaped in abstraction from or cut off from those other forms; and it is indispensably connected with warm affection or friendliness. Without such a connection we can find ourselves in an extremely dangerous void. Persons involved in this void feel helpless before internal and external realities which they carelessly allow to come into existence within and between themselves" (MO, 88-89). The last two sentences are an extremely accurate description of marital dysfunction.

Affirmation of the Person

This marital dysfunction is avoided or counteracted, according to my reading of this book, by the affirmation of the value of the person. This affirmation is no abstract "principle," but an active operation, a doing which is, in itself, a source of moral growth. In this operation the most fundamental value of the book is expressed.

Again it is worthwhile to quote the author at length: "In each situation in which we experience the sexual value of some person, love demands the integration or inclusion of that sexual value into the value of the person: this means the balanced integration of the sexual out of consideration for the value of the person. And it is precisely in this action that the fundamental trait of the ethics of love is expressed: love is affirmation of the person, and without such affirmation there is no love. If love has in it a specific response to the value of a person—here we have called this 'affirmation'—such love is, in the fullest sense, 'integral' love. If, on the other hand, 'love' is not pervaded by that affirmation of the value of the person, then it is a kind of dys-integral love, and not love at all. This is true even though the reactions and experiences of the people involved may have an exceedingly 'loving,' that is, erotic, character" (MO, 112).

The supportive and appreciative qualities of such a love are quite clear. But there is a deep spiritual quality which is essential to John Paul's viewpoint. Marital love is the creative unification of all human loves through the affirmation of the spirit of the persons. And by "spirit" I mean the principle of unity in human life. The integration of loves is a creative spiritual act. But it is also mutual in its creativity. Such mutuality is expressed in the couple's sense of belonging to each other.

Membership of Person to Person

The belonging of the couple *grows toward their becoming members of one another as persons*. These words are difficult but carefully chosen. In a sense this is the full outcome of an authentic affirmation of the other person. In brief, the affirmation cannot be detached, uninvolved, merely abstract. John Paul II has provided here a theological reflection on the proverb, "Where your *treasure* is, there also shall your heart be." He expresses this by the notion of a bodily joining and mutual *investment*. This process of joining, realizes the being of love, in the Pope's view, through "the deepest devotion of a loving person to the beloved." Here he finds the "specific weight" which distinguishes marital love from other less intense kinds. It is in the mutual affirmation of the value of two real persons joining their lives in a full commitment.

John Paul II sees the power of love operating in marriage as calling a person to cross the usual boundaries of the self. Rather than remaining within the person's natural untouchability and impregnability, love brings the person to actually wanting to give self to another, to the one that is loved. In his words, "It is as if it were a faculty of ecstasy—coming out from self in order to be more fully alive with the other. In no other form of love is this capacity realized in a manner so clear as in marital love" (MO, 114). This understanding of what happens in marital love likens it to a conversion transforming love of self into a special, sacramental form of love of neighbor. It changes a person's heart. "Marital love, a love of devotion," the Pope continues, "in an especially deep manner commits the will. Obviously, it is necessary here to dispose one's entire self, necessary to give one's soul, in the words of the gospel" (MO, 115).

In my opinion, it is this crossing of the boundaries of the self without losing the self which is the great challenge to married couples in our culture. I see it socially, in the churches, in my consulting room, and elsewhere. In many places we can observe desperate striving to do the works of love, especially through the sexual rubrics and rituals which fill the media marketplace. And yet it is striving without spirit, technique without commitment. Certain limited yet real satisfactions *can* be reached by technique, such as sensual pleasures. But John Paul II is saying that these must be taken into a full personal integration to find their lasting value. For technique alone is merely a form of use and, to quote the author, "Love cannot express itself in use alone, even if mutual and simultaneous. It expresses itself instead regularly in the union of persons. The fruit of this union is their mutual membership, of which the expression, among other things, is a full sexual life together; we call this mode of loving together conjugal communion, because in our view it properly takes place only in marriage" (MO, 115).

Limitations of space make it impossible to consider this book at greater length here. The work is unusually interesting and significant in providing detailed analysis of topics related to married life. They are topics which we don't ordinarily reflect on such as the process of using something, the subjective and objective sides of love, shame and guilt, providence and personal calling.

But again I want to remark that John Paul II is a very thorough philosophical writer. He does not reduce things to common sense but rather seeks to reveal the basis of what is taking place. In Polish, his book is difficult reading, and I could not imagine it being translated into easy English. But this book is worth working through, living with, and meditating or reflecting upon.

Love and Responsibility is what I would call, somewhat pedantically though not facetiously, a *seminal* book. The seeds for new possibilities and renewal exist within its pages.

Although I cannot accurately predict how well it will be received in America, I would not be surprised if the book had a positive impact on the pastoral care of married couples. I am sure, however, that my own ministry to married couples will benefit from John Paul II's insights.

Suggested Readings

Clinebell, Howard J., Jr. *Growth Counseling for Marriage Enrichment: Pre-Marriage and the Early Years.* Philadelphia: Fortress Press, 1975.

This is an interesting and practical book intended for pastors and couples. It is brief, to the point, and nontechnical. Emphasis is given to the human potential for growth through building relationships.

Clinebell, Howard J., Jr. and Charlotte H. *The Intimate Marriage.* New York: Harper & Row, Publishers, 1970.

A unified approach to the stages of marriage is presented by means of the experience of intimacy. The authors are well-known in Protestant circles for their work in pastoral care. Emphasis is given to the spiritual dimension of marriage.

Grunebaum, Henry, and Christ, Jacob, eds. *Contemporary Marriage: Structure, Dynamics, and Therapy.* Boston: Little, Brown and Company, 1976.

This is an anthology of articles by twenty-six authors intended for a professional audience. General areas covered are marriage and society, the structure and dynamics of marriage, and the treatment of marital problems. Highly recommended is the article "Learning to Work with Couples" by Lynn Parker Wahle.

Mace, David and Vera. *How to Have a Happy Marriage: A Step-by-Step Guide to an Enriched Relationship.* Nashville: Abingdon, 1977.

The Maces are the best known American couple working in the field of marriage counseling and enrichment. And this may be their most helpful book. It emphasizes practical exercises in communication and resolving conflicts. Excellent for guided couples' groups.

——————. *Marriage: East and West.* Garden City, New York: Doubleday & Company, 1960.

A classic cross-cultural study of marriage. This is very valuable in view of the increasing number of Asian-American marriages today.

——————. *We Can Have Better Marriages If We Really Want Them.* Nashville: Abingdon Press, 1974.

This book is helpful as an overview of the resources for marriage enrichment. It contains an extensive annotated bibliography.

Oates, Wayne. *Confessions of a Workaholic: The Facts About Work Addiction.* Nashville: Abingdon Press, 1971.

Although not about marriage, this book deals with a serious problem that afflicts many American marriages. In view of the growing number of two-income families, this *caveat* has become doubly important.

Pietropinto, Anthony, and Simenauer, Jacqueline. *Husbands and Wives: A Nationwide Survey of Marriage.* New York: Times Books, 1979.

This may be the most up-to-date, comprehensive, and informative resource on American marriages available. It covers why people marry, whom they choose, sex, relationship, conflict, infidelity, divorce, remarriage, and the future of marriage.

Rainer, Jerome and Julia. *Sexual Adventure in Marriage.* New York: Simon and Schuster, 1965.

This is a rather playful apology for sensuality in married life. The authors argue that our technological urban environment has deadened the senses of married couples. They suggest ways to cope with this situation. The book includes a considerable amount of interesting erotic literature.

Silverman, Hirsch Lazaar, ed. *Marital Therapy: Moral, Sociological and Psychological Factors.* Springfield, Illinois: Charles C. Thomas, Publisher, 1972.

Many diverse viewpoints are included in this classic anthology. It is valuable as a reference and includes the editor's very helpful summary of contributors' viewpoints and abstracts of their contributions.

Stewart, Charles William. *The Minister as Marriage Counselor.* Rev. ed. Nashville: Abingdon Press, 1970.

Some consider this to be the basic book on marriage counseling for pastors. It is somewhat dated but still helpful.

Viscott, David. *How to Live with Another Person.* New York: Arbor House, 1974.

Psychiatrist David Viscott presents a humanistic perspective on marriage. It presents some interesting ideas but does not develop them to any depth.